The Fool Sings

THE FOOL SINGS

poems by
Weslea Sidon

Rain Chain Press

Published by Rain Chain Press
Miami, FL

Book design: James Barrett-Morison

ISBN-13: 978-0-9888978-0-9
Copyright © 2014 Weslea Sidon
All rights reserved
Printed and bound in the United States of America

10 9 8 7 6 5 4 3 2 1

In loving memory of Florence Kaufman, who may not have liked all these poems, but would have loved that they were written.

Contents

ONE

I Keep Losing Things   11
Sea Breeze   12
Tenth Summer   14
Big Girl   15
Jamaica Bay, 1953   16
Coffee   18
In the ICU Waiting Room   20
The Last Sun of Broadway   21
Hands   22
The Goat Poems   24
Perigee Moon   28
The Bereavement Group Talks About Sex   29
Fog   30
In Her Grandmother's Room   32
Good Advice   33

TWO

The Fool Sings   37
All I Am Doing   38
The Singing Moon   39
Insomnia   40
Late Night Radio   42
Just Getting Home   43
All My Ideas Are Dead   44
Showers Likely in the North   45
Eve   46

Old Ones   47
At Miniature Golf   48
Razed   49
Spit Take   50
What She Said, Just Before Closing   51
The Writer Gives Up   52

THREE

Buying Ice Cream in an April Snow   57
How We Met   58
Barrow Street Window   59
Breakfast   60
Things Get Fixed   61
They Know You   63
After You Left   64
Afternoon Opera, Tremont, Maine   66
Blueberry Time   67
Rt. 102: Autumn Equinox   70
Rt. 102: 7AM, 3 Degrees   71
No One Here   72
Cabin Fever   73
Namaste   75
When The Waters Rise   76
Just Like You   77
Indian Summer   78
The Old Woman, Still in Love   79
Useful Information   80
Ants   82

ONE

I Keep Losing Things

I keep losing things
car keys, hats, paper cups
places on the page

I keep losing the sense of purpose
that propels me to the ends of sentences
I have lost the state of grace that comes
to those who know the plumber's number
or the limits of anticipation

I keep finding things that look like
reasons to continue looking
details masquerading as philosophy
I remember that these make a lie
but forget how many times
I've learned the lesson

Sea Breeze
on the 50th Anniversary of my mother's death

Alone on the cold beach
I am again the girl
with no history of comfort
telling myself the dark ocean
is consoling. Salt to salt,
drift to windblown drift.
In every bite of blowing sand
a memory of loss, a moment of denial.

Strength and suffering
are conjoined twins. Or so I was told
by my strong and suffering mother.
Hold your tears for something important,
hold your suffering like an amulet
against the temptation
to be happy and vacuous.

Loss after loss:
young husband, young friends,
little body parts that one can live without.
Years of tearless days, long nights
of traitorous sobs.

White caps, mist spray
break from waves beneath.
At last I can want the wide arms of sea breeze
filled with salt, roses, heather, to encircle
like the soft arms of a sturdy old aunt.

Wave by wave
the bond of strength and suffering devolves
exposing another shore, sad but safe
where a weeping girl can breathe
deep, deep in.

Tenth Summer

The lifeguard is striding toward us.
He is so tan, so full of his own
loveliness, his long lashes
just missing his creamed-white nose.

He stands ready to climb the short ladder
and we are all ready,
party to deception, girls pretending
no one is watching them watch him.

We have no idea what it would feel like
to find a mouth near our mouth
under the creamy nose,
but we are sure it will be enough.

He looks cool in hot sun:
cool as the ocean wave
that sploshes over us
letting us forget he's even there.

Big Girl

She liked to hang around the big girls, the tough girls.
They called her squeaky, the mascot, the kid,
let her listen until their talk turned sexy
and they sent her home.

She hoarded their words,
she hoarded the laughter, and the slouch.
They tweaked her hair,
lank brown clumps unevenly divided into tails.

She took the colors of their lipsticks into bed,
saw the insides of her eyelids glow
Glamour Pink, Hot Shot Red.
She practiced the sneer, the stroll,
learned to cover matches in the wind.

They let her light their smokes
called her skinny-wig, bug-eye,
they painted up her lips with Autumn Plum
then laughed and laughed.

They told her she had bird legs
which meant she'd never have
big boobs, and laughed.

So she laughed, too, and called herself
sneaky squeak, pin-ankle, baby boob,
until the big girls laughed so much
that even when their talk turned
really sexy they didn't send her home.

Jamaica Bay, 1953

1.
Our road had not yet
given up its secret.

We could drive away
from the new six-story boxes
that grew in empty lots
where once only shorebirds lived,
and old cars died
away from the river
to the creek
where shanties held
damp mysteries in patchwork shingles

we could sit beside the speckled dunes
and wait for the murmuring tide.

2.
We let our fingers drag behind the rowboat
swirling slips of marsh grass
trying to spell our names.

Our names washing out to sea,
and soon the smiles of our young parents
erased by hospitals and surgeons.

But not quite yet. There is, for now
the sunlit island so small our jumpings
make it bounce—and we are jumping
loping side-wise after horseshoe crabs
tossing bits of crusty sandwich to the gulls.

3.
I float beneath the cloudless ancient sky
seaweed woven to a wreath around each wrist.
My eyelids droop and close, I have no fear
of water, nor of solitude.
I have yet to learn how small I am
how little I can do.

Coffee

    A mistake at the deli
gets me my mother's coffee:
'regular,' normal once, in that time
when sweet and light and regular
were what life should be.

    I drink mine black,
bitter, machismo.
I laugh when people wince
as if I never longed to be
soothed by creamy sweetness,
by thickened normalcy
hanging behind my teeth
like crinolines.

    I'm too impatient
now, at the deli, to think about this
or about my warm dark
mother sitting in the kitchenette,
back to tiny window,
sending irregular curls of cigarette smoke
into a dance of swans and geese
rising with steamed milk
in her numbered mornings,
believing in her dying
that her bitter daughter
would lighten, someday
trust sweetness, be soothed.

I asked for black.
The counter woman nods
but sighs as she takes the cup
as if she sees what I will not remember,
will not hold onto
long enough
to taste.

In the ICU Waiting Room

a television batters the angry silences
the sad silences   the fears of silence

we sit in the oddly grouped chairs
chrome arms too high to allow
a hand to cross in comfort
low tables are piled with magazines
on travel, wildlife, cars
escape they say, leave your sorrow
leave your shame, leave your sick

a phone rings   a question is answered
a question is posed   doctors hurry away

natant voices rise to the surface
speak their mantras of hope or denial
sink beneath the TV's flicker and drone

The Last Sun of Broadway

The last sun of Broadway
clung like honey to the apples
rows of apples curling onto the street
where she thought she once lived
slices curled onto plates before her
somewhere
she reached
brown spotted fingers hovered above flawless fruit
she reached
a glass bowl sparkled, somewhere
she remembered
thou shalt not
remembered the voice of god
thou shalt not
remembered until only god was there
curling around her
clinging like honey
as she told him of apples
told him until she slept
spread like honey
on the street
dreaming of apples
and of God
who said no more.

Hands
for Kent Sidon

1973
the palm of my
husband's hand is heavy
in my palm
the weight of all we will
not do, have never done
right, pressing
into my waiting fingers
the only part of us
still alive

1974
under the antiseptic
each hospital corridor
has its own smell
disease or desperation
or one nurse's laundry
detergent, after a while
you know your own enough
to let it guide you
when your eyes won't focus
and the elevator is the only
place you dare to keep them
closed, after a while you
find it home, on your hairbrush
on the cat, on every thing you touch
or try to wipe away

1975
I have not slept in weeks
so what, I keep telling my body,

when he dies you will sleep for days
a year if you have to
if you sleep now he will call
and you will not answer
he will be
afraid

I fill a syringe
drawing back the plunger
pressing out an air bubble
that could kill, that could
end the pain the drugs
will block for a few hours

the nurse who taught me
how to give the shots at home
told me I was a good wife,
good with my hands, I said
but I wasn't even that

1976
my left hand dances across
the frets of Kent's guitar
like cartoon sprites leaping
in glittering glens
I am surprised, my playing
is not always light, never
smooth, the frail guitar
buzzes and rattles against
my chest, but its tone still
clings to the air like the
scent of honeysuckle

The Goat Poems

> *Scholarship, in its concern with the history of ideas, shows how easily genuine elements of knowledge can combine with illusory notions to form grandiose systems of thought in which the mind is content to dwell for a time.*
>   Encyclopedia Britannica

1. In The Gallery

woman 1: why does she do goats
       2: why does anybody do anything
       3: look at this! quick! this is the pink
         in my wallpaper

2. At The Fair

kids—
each side of the fence
has a small face, grinning
tiny bit of nose
strong enough to knock open the gate
nuzzles into a hand
too small and weak to close it

3. In The Sky

they were all Capricorns
husband, best friend, persistent former lover
possessing never mentioned similarities
that I catalogued and counted

and would not ascribe to stars

    he all wire and spring
    she sleek, with dark crescent smile
    the other round and horned

and I, Cancer, Moon-child spinning in their midst
fighting gravity I would not ascribe to stars
clinging to each
shedding no light
finding no orbit

then, of a piece, they were gone

    he dead
    she absent on funeral day, fleeing
    the other deciding it was no time for casual advances

and I, dark moon in an empty sky
spun without heat
touched nothing, felt nothing
moved past supermarket shelves
and new-love smiles as if they were the same
grew heavy and sank under the weight
of absent stars

4. At The Fair

    a ferris wheel turns
under the dimpled moon
shameless squeals descend
we watch the slow turning

cars become rings of blue
light, pink light, yellow
laughter billowing out
shimmering

   embarrassed to show
the little boy I am afraid
to let him ride
I tell him
it is time to watch the goats
get their blue ribbons, time
to see the feeding,
learn something about
nature as if it wasn't nature's
pure delight squealing as it
lifted free

5. In The Gallery

the pink goat turns
to the shimmering corner
plump moon rising off center
tethered to canvas
by the dark crescent smile

the women turn silent
whys and wallpapers swallowed
they jostle the fence
between looking and seeing

   what is to be seen
in the smile of a goat

what is to be known of the
grinner grinning back

if I learn what is known in the blood
will I see blood billow toward the
silvered sky, will it rise and shimmer
like laughter will it fall like shooting stars
if I tell what I know
will I smile

Perigee Moon

the spent glower of an old cat
lingers, yellow, in the opal night
ivy rustles with a squirrel's leap
from locust to dead sassafras
to wizening hemlocks, to air

    my mother would have liked this yard
    considered it a proper fit,
    cleaned it up without asking
    permission but without complaint,
    sat in the rubble and told
    some racy anecdote
    that would twist and tangle
    like berry hedge
    buffering evanescent truths
    against the winds
    of fact and fiction

    we must have seen the moon together
    when she took me out at dawn
    to walk off my insomnia,
    when we followed frozen streams
    to twilight haunts
    but I have no memories
    no sagas of her winter skies,
    still it is this sky that brings her

perigee moon scattering reflections
through ivy, through hemlock
chill air exposing a tenderness
long withheld, lingering now
almost within reach

The Bereavement Group Talks About Sex

Two years after he died
she came back to the field
they had last walked as lovers.

For decades
touch had been their sport and refuge
hands, lips always finding new delights
in old passion.

She could sense him now,
his steady arm holding her
the first time she raised
her timid lips to his,
the last time as she raised her eager mouth
to shush the laughter above his silver beard.

She could sense him too soon after,
the illness souring his lips
his fingers pushing hers away
closing each button she opened
refusing even memory of ecstasy.

She came back to the field to see
if the stand of lupin
had held the shape of her memories
long enough to give them back,

if love left a trail
that she could follow forward
even as it closed behind.

Fog

This morning
I can not see
the garden from the porch.
I try to remember the rows
    squash, beans, carrots, dill
I am not sure.

I am not sure
I can remember your face
What I see is a picture
    you, standing in the roadway
    waving
    looking elsewhere.

If I walk
I can push back the fog
    porch to fence
    fence to woodpile
    wood to garden.

Is there a path to your face:
    fingers to forearm
    forearm to shoulder
    shoulder to neck?
I am not sure.

I am not sure
I can find what is knowable
by way of what is known.

This morning I can not see
the porch from the garden.

In Her Grandmother's Room

The last thing she found was an apron
balled tight and stuffed behind the stove,
pitiful strings crinkled,
a weight of sooty grease welding
the fabric to the floor.

This meticulous kitchen—
each drawer relined each year,
each bit of linen refolded to ward off
the curse of crease—
where no one dared to spill,
or sigh as a cup of bitter tea
followed a stifled tale of heart break
down the drain. A drop of honey, a drop of anger
both invited vermin.

No one would have seen her yank the perfect bow,
wrench some crushing pain from kitchen sanctuary
and stuff it in a winding sheet of flowering percale.
She saw her now, but only rising afterward
turning to select another apron from a scented drawer.
She saw her smooth the apron front, and one or two
bold strands of hair, then let the kitchen door swing
shut behind her, silent on its gleaming hinge.

Good Advice

it's not enough to break them you said
you need a beat
you need to hear the bottles shatter
the way a bell breaks up in reverb

to get it right, you said
you need pulse   get the bottles
smashing so they ring against the sink
bells in reverb shattering the air

think about your blood
pulsing through your veins
think about your heart, you said
pumping all that blood

think about your heart, you said
think about the way it shattered
about the way the beats
echoed in the halls of the hospital

shattered and beating, you said
even when you wished you could make it stop
when the blood in your heart was so cold
you could have been stone

it's ok, you said
to get the bottles smashing
hear them break up   hear them shatter
what is left of that air

TWO

The Fool Sings

1.
Wind is blowing and the moon is full.
Cold, at last, is crossing the water, riding the wind
in a chariot of icicles, gold in the sun.
I would be a fool to let it in.

2.
Slipshod plastic billows under Christmas lights.
The moon has multiplied itself,
but only if I lie beneath the window looking up,
seeing upside down.

3.
Fierce moon,   righteous wind
slender plastic,   narrow bed.
Warmth is an assumption;
cold is a fact.

4.
Stars in the water,   moon light on straw
faces appear in the window until breath
blows them out.

5.
Only a fool would open the door
to smell the stars, to feel the moon
to breathe the fierce and righteous night
to ride the narrow icebound wind
above the field of straw.

All I Am Doing

All I am doing is driving
singing loudly with Aretha
sock it to me sock it to me
sock it to me sock it to me
thinking about time
that goes nowhere
nowhere
which is where I'm driving
trying to stop thinking about time

I see a shoe here and there
remember why one foot was out
and no one felt the shoe go
I see a dog
empty face
understanding why I do not stop

crazy people walk the shoulders
old women from another time
pick dandelion greens
dogs die and are left for later
I'm singing
sock it to me sock it to me sock it to me
thinking about time
how it's always tailgating
bearing down with rude headlights
no matter what speed I'm going

time
is now 9:57
I'm driving
        singing something else

The Singing Moon
in memory of Crystal Star

the singing moon
her troubled eyes
cast down beneath arched brows
her round and tender mouth
held firm against the sorrowed sound
woeful echo of pleading sun
calls   look up   look up
I sing for you

> *I pierce the husk of deafening shadow*
> *slake the blinding silence*
> *chime the hardened churl of sadness*
> *chime your hidden heart*

the singing moon beckons
languorous hum of water
lulls the restless shore
but the path of nubbled silver
will not wait   she draws it back
calls   do not send your body
send your song

> *syllable by syllable*
> *unloose your shroud of secret longing*
> *keen above the fugue of ocean*
> *until the voices of your sorrow*
> *ring within the sacred cordatura of my light*

Insomnia

1.
trace the edges of
the dream, run
a damp finger, blur
the seams, cut one
fraying moment from
the whole, start again

trace the edges of
the dream, slice each
fraying moment at
the quick, leave the
sullen light to blur
outside, start again

trace the edges of
the dream, drape
the arching fingertips
of day, damp the
raucous drone
blur the seams
start again

2.
dreamer
ride your silken sleep
down the icy yellow sky
round the smiles
that ring you in

through the whirlpool's
scarlet eye

snare nightmare
in the warp of night
winnow sense from sign
suck the purling moon breath in
dance the incubus beyond
the realms
of sanguinary lullaby.

3.
I woke up laughing
sleep beached in unfamiliar light

jagged bits of voice
clinging to a shattered dream

jagged bits of dream
repeating broken voice

you can not mend a night
rent by shards of vision

you can not laugh
the light back

no light can
hold the night back

Late Night Radio

On back roads flanked by pines that glower and growl
flickerings of wild eyes pull your gaze into thickets
so tangled they'd never find you—
not in winter, blackened skin just one more shadow of a stump
under clean, clean snow
not in spring when you stank
in the thaw.

The radio won't give you anything but
late night preachers praying you'll go off
with only your pro-choice bumper sticking out of the wreck,
and Connie Francis singing Home On The Range
young and silly enough to be sad except slime from the motel
where she got raped is oozing on a hairpin turn ahead.
Let go of the wheel to change the station and you'll
spin out so fast your howl will reach the satellite.
Just one more country nut they'll say,
tuning you out.

Even inside the car
your body feels like it's on a kite string
just above the asphalt
held by someone who might think it's funny to let go.
You can hear them laughing as you swivel and flutter
damning yourself for wearing bright red flannel,
so pretty in the wind.

Just Getting Home

Ice outside the front door
is pitted and discolored
but firm, unyielding.

Within the boundaries of the orchard
ice has dominion: woodpeckers pound;
rabbits leave faint tracks
in the dust of new snow,
quiet on sheer ground.

In sun, ice and snow
are brilliants, bound by silver shadows
encircling a world of wind and cold.

There is nothing else:
A gust, a drift, unfettered snow;
ice bound stairs as insurmountable as glaciers
and a door
beyond a solid sea.

All My Ideas Are Dead

their corpses lie about
the garden or float around me
making ghastly demands

a few show signs of struggle
bashed in the oddest places
full of holes innards exposed

a few are finely dressed
on their way to cocktails
or a tea dance in the pergola

I riffle the pockets
of a shop-worn suit
looking for a change of heart

I lift a sequined hem
in hope an inspiration
was hidden there for safety

a diamond-clad
dismembered hand drops by
gives me the finger

at night I hear them singing
phantom songs

Showers Likely in the North

I listen to the weather as if to war news:
    four, five times a day
showers   continuing   showers.

The water smokes and beyond the water land is hidden.
    Land does not disappear;
appears to disappear is not the same.

Words smoke and beyond the words a sense is hidden.
    Sanity can disappear;
appears to reappear is not the same.

No sentence makes an island rise through rain, through smoke;
no island makes a sentence gather sun above dead water.

No words appear to stop the rain.

Eve

Eve putters in her new garden
the one she had to plant herself,
the one she had to rake and hoe
and turn, while Adam scorned her
aching back as mental imbalance
caused by pregnancy.

Now she tickles the baby's belly
with soft weeds
and lifts the toddler
above the spongy rows.

Adam mutters that he's tired
and hungry and knows the soup
is burning.

Eve doesn't miss the old garden,
fruit falling squishy and rank
before she got to choose.
Grasses hiding path and pit,
Adam fat with authority—
a bureaucrat with large desk
and empty drawers.

She doesn't mind the work.
It soothes to be tired
from soil and sun;
she coddles her patience
waits for her seedlings to show.

Old Ones

When did we become the joke:
    the blonde painting in two coats,
    the moron on the roof waiting for his drink.

No one will speak to us in the bar:
    not the 12-inch pianist
    not the grasshopper named Bill.

We are not going to be met in the Spring
    even if we get through the mattress.

Nobody believes we can
    screw
    in so much
    as a light bulb.

No one will come to the door,
    not even to ask "Who's there?"
    when we knock.

At Miniature Golf

Bent over castle turrets
my glance can bounce
from roof tops to towers,
to the slim upper hems
of countryless flags.

My hands can gather a flowered field,
one step will cross the mountain,
straddle the moat,
one sigh will push a windmill arm
through the sullen air.

Oh to be the giant:
the thunder over village huts,
the shadow on the sun;

the keeper of the cave,
the tinkling steeple bell,
the stalwart plastic tree.

Razed

now that the ghost of Captain Latty has no house,
no cellar door to open in a rush of cold
no springs to squeak on rusty beds
no steps to creak between
attic dusk and basement dawn

now that he is hidden in the empty air
unable to shift invisible bulk into a grown girl's dream
or rattle windows soaking up September sun
like a jilted suitor desperate to get in

now that he is memory and myth
dismissible except that he both lived and died
it seems unfair that he might be alone
with nothing but an outcropped stone
and one bent tree

now that Captain Latty
casts no shadow in the empty hall
I'm certain it was never me
hissing into vacant rooms
insisting he was never there

Spit Take

At the old bar in the Chinese take-out
on the corner, by the railroad
you heard this guy telling
the kind of jokes that made Jewish you
want to go to Confession,
because you needed
forgiveness after laughing so hard
at those mean and ugly jokes,
those mean and ugly and funny, funny jokes.

You needed someone to tell you
it wasn't so bad that you laughed until
you did a spit take with the hot and sour soup,
that you had to grab the table with both hands to keep
from sliding under, that you could never
press your knees together hard enough
to stop the inevitable pee.

And now, you're laughing
because here's another old bar
in another Chinese take-out that reminds you
how you couldn't stop the laughing,
reminds you how even now
that foul-mouthed bastard
could get you, any time.

What She Said, Just Before Closing

I am getting too old to die young
passing the point where people mourn
what lay ahead, what lay ahead is lying
like old dishes in the sink
scummy with traces of yesterday.

I would mourn my own youth if I remembered it.
The one I invented is somber enough
smoky and smudged with tear-dragged mascara
(stolen from dime stores or found on a train)
the one I invented splatters its factoids
all over the truth,
leaving a hole if you rub out the stain
leaving a maze of revisions, deletes,
leaves you assumptive, well sated with answers
glad to get out.

I might fear tomorrow
but why waste it
by the time it's over I'll have decided
how to tell it, relive the good parts,
happened or not, shed tears for the tragic,
whoever's, no matter, I'll get over it
I've lived long enough
to know how.

The Writer Gives Up

I heat my house with mail.
I know by the color of the flame
if it is accept or reject
manuscripts burn anyway
the new ones and the old
are written mailed and burned.

I wear shoes that sound like ducks
childhood ducks, wallpaper ducks
I can not get far
but then, I do not go out.

The pockets of my coat are full
of onomatopoeia that didn't work
and a scarf the color of a burning poem
crumpled concerns are mistaken
for dollars and vice versa
neither buys a word I don't already have.

THREE

Buying Ice Cream in an April Snow

Sometimes it's easier to stop.

So we stopped,
watched the insistent
green of April glow through
late snow, watched the sky
open and close and open
watched the counter girl
scoop and press and pull
lingered
between chosen and unchosen cold
until it was easier to go on.
And we went on

How We Met

Suppose I decided to tell a different version
of that day, now after all these years of
sticking to one story, after all the retellings
at dinner tables (apologies to those who have heard)

the decorated facts, always the same.
Suppose you couldn't recognize the thread of truth
that laced the string of words that rolled
by rote into our custom made passion play.
Suppose I rooted our life in different soil
grafted different limbs onto our tree
placed our garden elsewhere, dumped the
rotted mold of doubt over well-tended borders.

Suppose we got past the obvious—mischief, madness
would our life unravel like a loose-knit hat,
would we stumble down the precipice of maybes
pulling primordial what ifs behind us like tinker toys,

would we swirl in separate eddies,
drown in specious undercurrents,
would we bubble to the surface, bloated, purple strangers
meant to meet again?

Barrow Street Window

When the sudden chill hits the street
we watch an old woman pull her collar high,
cup her dog against her chest
explaining about wind, about cold.

Next door
the pianist works on "Summertime"
& the livin is, the livin is,
he misses the dissonance
reaches for it, misses.
Accidental sweetness
hangs in the wall between us

> accidental sweetness
> like the time you said I love you
> mid-sex
> and love, an accident,
> took hold in our lives.

Even inside we pull collars tight
the lies of March
brightened by wind,
the lies of love
still sweetening the air.

The old woman
holds the trembling dog
hush little, hush.
The pianist reaches,
you shiver
and move away.

Breakfast

If you have nothing to say say nothing,
she says, thinking it's coquettish,
an echo of times when pronouncements
seemed simply true
instead of ridiculous.
This is not what he hears.
This has a rasp, a hiss;
it charges the air
cracks open a fault line.
He slams the table,
her empty cup rattles in mocking rhythm
against an unmatched saucer.
His coffee spills—
skim-milk gray, dead man gray—
a slick veneer solid for an instant
then a pitted landscape of rivulets and mud.
They watch it drip
each fixed on different floor tiles.
She still holds an unused napkin,
his chair scrapes,
his footprints smear,
they say nothing.

Things Get Fixed

she watched him slither out
  lean legs misleading under his puffy middle
    waiting for the little grin of satisfaction
      he always had when he tied the muffler up
        his job well done

it wasn't there

she was ready
  with her own half-hearted good-job lie
    that sounded like a lie, that sounded
      like a lie from someone trying to be kind

she was waiting to say it
  when his lean leg kicked the fender
    slamming   slamming   screaming

I hate this ratty car, I hate our rotten ratty life,

  a storm
    of truths/half-truths
      a detonation of necessary little lies

        of their dangling, dragging life
          tied up like the muffler with bits of shredded love

            with habits of calm satisfaction
            with ritual kindness

she didn't know how long she watched
  he didn't know how long he kicked

lost in the storm, watching the fender
  crumple in slow motion
    hearing his screed whip and bend
      and break the lies
        the lovely cautions of their security

he stopped
  grabbed his burning foot and fell
    against the steady silent car

she waited
  praying what came next
    would be as good

They Know You

they know you
know if they smile and keep talking
you'll smile and keep listening
until there they are
    with the last ticket to the late show
    the window seat
    the only pair of 7½s in red

they know you
know if they smile and keep moving
you'll smile and keep signaling
until they are
    in your spot
    the one in front of the exit
    the one that's good until Monday

they know you
know how long it takes you to smile
before you say something
which is just how long they need to smile
and disappear

After You Left

I thought about
the twenty-year-old lover
I had when I was
twenty.
He had a mother
I called Mrs.
a shadow I avoided.

I gathered up
coffee cups, swept crumbs
tried to feel
frumpy,
as if I hadn't seen
it coming, or started
wearing perfume into
class.

I wondered if
I would call your
mother Mrs. if I
met her on the street,
and why I didn't mention
that your books
were still in the kitchen.

After you left

I played three songs
on the piano.

I forgot the words
to two, and never
found the key
for the other,
but
it was such a relief
to be wrong.

Afternoon Opera, Tremont, Maine

Behind me, on the radio
a mythical Prague is burning.
A soprano laments with joyful competence,
a smallish robin in the yard turns
to look our way.

I am told the robin hunts by sound,
that worms beneath the surface
can be heard.   I love this information
too much to find out if it is true.

What does the soprano, loud
and buoyant, signal in the open air?
Do worms beneath the robin know
camouflage? Will the robin hear the worms
take cover in the melismatic triumph of the song?

Ahead of me the tide is covering
the salt flats. The burnished ledge
has taken on the purple cast of distant hills at twilight.
Prague, on lifts and casters, grows dim.
Soprano and robin leave their stages
hushed.

Blueberry Time

1.
up the road the early rakers stoop
strong thighs low
to the gentle slope

the rolling lilt of berries
soft scraped against the rakes
not yet pierced by late morning
shouts teasing complaints

dawn lingering
sky still the color of gravestones
berry blue and leaf green
hidden from the road by mist

2.
inside a new chain link fence
a small community of dead
    names still known to those
    who leave plastic flowers
    and flags on holidays
lures the jogging couple
    allowed to dawdle on vacation
who find the plastic quaint
who read the flags naive
the stones romantic

they are feeling good
about themselves and sorry

for the dead who did not have
sex at 5 AM with sea smoke
almost in their bed
before they knew the dawn run
would be perfect before they saw
themselves recounting the darling
cemetery to their friends before
they saw the rakers
and began to argue whether
labor was noble
or inane

3.
the waitress
gazes over the blueberry barrens
and counts weeks till frost
when the last of these couples
will be someplace, anyplace else

she recognizes these two
she saw them in the little cemetery
this morning when she brought breakfast
to her daughter on the raking crew
they were laughing, waving one of the flags

now they've ransacked the menu
taken the number 6 and asked for
substitution after substitution until
the 6 is gone. She won't bother to tell them
they've ended up with a number 10
change is their point, getting the better
of a breakfast shop

but she has a well-practiced
been here my whole life twinkle
so they end up with blueberry pancakes,
because she says the crop is the best ever
and they always like to have the best

4.
August sun
clear light the color of warm butter
washes over varnished table tops
sizzles over the barrens
catches every silver sparkle
in the granite stones

frost
the waitress thinks
will take her daughter back to college
raking money stuffed in her back pack
rippling muscles aching under her jeans

frost will take the waitress
back to high school
teaching math to earnest freshmen
who know her well enough to tease
about adding up the breakfast checks

by then the berry leaves will redden
to a sweet grenadine
turning summer's end into persistent sunset
indigo shadows of the chain link fence
dissolving into mist

Rt. 102: Autumn Equinox

I am glad, for once, to be staid and slow,
stuck in the wake of this lagging truck
hauling a crusty boat, dragging summer with it.

Leaves have made their turn away from green,
not all, enough to goad the mice indoors,
enough to catch one's breath beside the lake.

Our old road dips and curves away from south,
begins the western loop, the shorter side, the steeper side.
Away from town the road is empty
but for us: the patient, the slow.

The lowering sun is blinding; the pick-up rattles
over crackled heaves, the old boat shivers.
I lower my gear, drop back,
brace for the shuddering climb.

Rt. 102: 7 AM, 3 Degrees

Ghostly now,
a full moon hoards the rays of rising sun:
lovers moving into realms apart
reluctant to be free.

Elusive moon
lowering from tree tops,
long branches dripping with silken snow,
dense and welcome sun ascending
from the lobster shack to the peak of my neighbor's house.
The peak, ragged with shingled ice
looming between sun and ocean.

You, my hero of the morning,
champion of the coffee pot, finder of the lost watch
have given me lunch and words of caution;
taken back the bed.

On the path snow squeaks, ice groans.
Sea smoke hovers above empty moorings;
scrapings from the windshield of my waiting car
flurry away toward the setting moon.

The road is clear.

No One Here

I'm new
and no one here wants to know me better

but I keep hoping,
dangling car keys and shifting feet
to avoid the looks that tell me
to stop talking and get going.

A guy who just arrived with beer
has passed a bottle to his host.
His wife pours herself a glass.
No one offers me any;
our tension aggravates like smog.

The sting of small town life eluded me so far,
loneliness seemed soft:
a carpet draped
between my old life and my new.

My car, at least, is warm
and loud enough to say I'm really gone.
The sky is dense and threatening
even so I take the longest road home.

Cabin Fever

These are hard nights.
I stand and gape at the dim horizon,
at a snow-laden pine that recedes
from shape to shadow,
at the narrowing thread that told of sun.

On starless nights I miss the city streets.
I miss the bus that ran on Nostrand Avenue
all night, all weather; I miss the lights
on upper floors, the lights put on, turned off
by strangers moving in familiar ways.

I miss the radiator hissing and clanging
like a grand old kettle on a grand old stove.
I miss the street lamp
mistaken for the rising moon,
long after we knew east from west.

These are hard nights. The cold is mean;
the dark is menacing. Ice hides beneath
the gleaming snow and sorrow, demon strong,
feasts on a memory of ever-lit streets full
any hour, every hour with people never
stopped by weather.

So what, if busses didn't come
and bladed rain burned through a light coat,
if there was wet skin, ruined plans,

lonely hours at the window looking out
on traffic lights with no one stopped, no one going.

In moonless, starless gloom, beset by demons
frozen huge in frigid air I miss the stories I read
in far off windows on upper floors: fairy tales
where everyone was warm, everyone was dressed
(no blubbery coats, no earring-eating hats)
and everyone had a reason to be out.

Namaste

In Yoga, hands in prayer position,
I sense some ancient gene begin to feel sacrilegious.
The Jews don't do this. The ancestor Jews
who are rarely concerned with my daily life
have decided to be confrontational
about prayer position.   This is how it is lately—
they show up, they don't mince words, they aren't logical.
They have a way, these ancestor genes,
of sounding like they know something I don't, so
here and there they catch me at a disadvantage. After all,
how righteous can this old agnostic be when she's about
to fart in wind-reliever pose, or is having a small epiphany
concerning toenail polish and the correctness of blue
on her classmate's feet.

But there is no time here to be concerned,
no pose long enough to ruminate.
I hold my hands in front of my heart,
as I have been asked to do, and pray,
which I have not been,
to be forgiven my transgressions
or be left the hell alone.

When The Waters Rise

My love, the gulf of sadness
has swallowed you. You drift,
your bones too tired to bear
the weight even of skin;
skin too tired to fend off heat or cold.

Specters foul your ears,
every word becomes a spear
hurled from a fortress of mockery.

Love, try to see me, try to hear me,
touch my hand and know: I am here.
Please, believe I am here.

When this tide ebbs,
when you can safely stand,
we will stroll the edge of this vast beach
to see how close to the horizon you have been;
how well you have made it back.

We will keep watch.
We will be ready
when the waters rise again.

Just Like You

I remind myself
how good it is to be alone
pausing to notice
how much like you I look
in the dark windows,
how well your old shirt
suits these jeans.

How good to hear my own thoughts
without the drone of small talk, I say
reaching for the radio.
But the DJ sounds just like you
such a coincidence, I can not turn him off.

I take all the blankets
shape them to myself
rest a cup of tea
where yesterday I rubbed your shoulder
strew the books I have waited to read in solitude
across the length of bed
and stare into the television
wondering why I never noticed
that the weatherman
looks just like you.

Indian Summer

We found them all
as we remembered:
the rocky path to shore,
the place of fallen trees,
the sometime island in the cove,
fringed with autumn gold
but otherwise the same.

Still we were surprised
to hear our laughter echo
to think of lying undone
on the bluffs;
to know the breath of
summer's past would
blow hot again
before it smoked
with frost.

The Old Woman, Still in Love

This is what I have come to know:
god was once an aging woman
wondering who would care if
she had one more
beer in front of the tube,
or another mint, or
another man.

Everyone tries to get away
somedays
without brushing their teeth,
or putting the last quarter in the meter.
This is not to say
honesty and hygiene have lost their relevance,

only that they matter less
than the way we savor the guilt
of warm cherry pie,
your arm under mine
as we carry it home.

Useful Information
inspired by the back of a marbleized notebook

1. Table of Multiplication

one nasty word
times ten nasty words
equals ten horrible days
of zero words.

2. Table of Weights & Measures (Dry)

One grain of sand has more
weight than any desire to be good.
One ounce of desire has more mass
than any pound of intentions.
No number of tons of fond wishes
weighs more than a grain of despair.

3. Table of Liquid Measure

All blood that to and from the heart moves
in polyrythmic sequence can not dilute
the two swift tears that fall
as you leave. Gallons
of tears, barrels of tears, hogsheads
of tears spilled into flowered pools under
branching junipers could not fill
the half-round dent
on your side of the bed.

4. Table of Paper Measure

24 sheets equal   1 quire.
Blank or covered,   1 quire.
Insipid or grand,   1 quire.
True or untrue,   1 quire.

5. Table of Circular Measure

If it is a true circle the end
of the end and the beginning
of the beginning will be
indistinguishable. If the diameter
of a love song is longer
than the melody of its existence
the song will be unresolved.
If every degree of infinite
regret stood end to end
around the equator, not one
could exceed 69.19 miles.

6. Table of Miscellaneous Measure

Whether you wait sixty seconds
or walk sixty seconds
it will still be a minute.
Whether or not you return
it will still be a minute.

Ants

An ant has made his way
across a slender bit of chaff
and is debating choices:
another bit of chaff,
green heart of violet leaf,
my shoe?

He does not waver because his relatives
came across the ocean in a rotted mast,
or survived a garden holocaust.

He does not care if his queen
is toxically neurotic.
He does not care that his family tree
is rife with incest and cannibalism.

Survival is all.
That, and a taste
for my salty feet.

Acknowledgments

These poems, sometimes in different form, previously appeared in the following publications: *Bangor Metro* ("Afternoon Opera, Tremont, Maine"); *Gulf Stream Magazine* ("All I Am Doing," "Barrow Street Window," "The Goat Poems," and "I Keep Losing Things"); *The New York Times* Metropolitan Diary ("Buying Ice Cream in an April Snow"); *Off the Coast* ("Breakfast" and "Eve"); *Salonika* ("Hands," "Insomnia," and "Jamaica Bay"); *Two With Water* ("Coffee"); *Wolfmoon* ("Razed"); *Xanadu* ("Blueberry Time," "The Last Sun of Broadway," and "Perigee Moon"); *Z Miscellaneous* ("They Know You").

"Afternoon Opera, Tremont, Maine" was reprinted in and "Rt. 102: Autumn Equinox" appeared in *Still On The Island* (Crooked Road Press, 2009). "In Her Grandmother's Room" appeared in *From the Porch Swing* (Silver Boomer Books, 2010). "Buying Ice Cream In An April Snow" was reprinted in *The Bar Harbor Times*. "Fog" appeared in *Paumanok* (Cross-Island Communications, 2009). "Tenth Summer" appeared in *Paumonak Interwoven* (Island Sound Press, 2013).

I am indebted to many people for their help in seeing this book to completion. Listing each of them would be impossible, but thank you all, just the same. For unconditional faith and the occasional swift kick in the tush, thank you to: Curtis Wells, Margo Hirsch, Ingrid Hughes, The Poetry Nerds, members of the Long Island Poetry Collective, Ellie Pancoe, The W.O.W. group, and all the students who have demanded that I practice what I preach.
W.S.

www.ingramcontent.com/pod-product-compliance
Lightning Source LLC
Chambersburg PA
CBHW020702300426
44112CB00007B/477